Pink Poems
Tan Thoughts

D1617549

By: Sinai Cota

Pink Poems Tan Thoughts
Stories and illustrations by Sinai Cota

Published by Sinai Cota

ISBN: 9798648950771

To my readers:

I wrote this book for you; so that you never feel alone again; so when pain shows up your first thoughts are to heal and not hurt; so that sharing your story brings relief and power and that my words can awaken within you strength that can never be taken away.

Contents

Preword:

The Dating Diary of a Brown Girl

I'm a brown girl that grew up with light skin on the opposite side of the Mexican border believing in fairy tales that taught me: white was better and more beautiful. It was the blue-green eyes in my barbie dolls, as a little girl, and the pale complexion in the men I dated, that convinced me to sacrifice my language and traditions as a young adult to be a part of their world and make believe a fairy tale of my own.

But when that illusion faded, a little Brown girl emerged from the storybook with her own magic, eager for an adventure of her own whilst still believing in true love's kiss (if there ever was such a thing).

So here lies *mi verdad*: my journey healing from trauma, engaging in self-love and forging new beginnings. I hope these words ahead encourage you to reflect in your own story and to embrace the good, the bad and the ugly- because WE are our own authors. WE have the power to shift the stories before us now and always.

Shades of Brown

You wrap yourself in college
degrees, like armor to protect
you from the world, as if the
color of your skin won't be a
topic for conversation.

When they say "I don't see
color", you uncomfortably
smile and nod, feeling
invisible once again because
they just said, "I don't see
you".

They underestimate your
power.

Meanwhile you're quietly
and fiercely paving the way
for more of us- the Brown
bodies they don't see.

We will be seen. And they'll
wonder how we got here...
because we were so quiet.

Our presence will thunder
loud and proud, in sync to
the rhythm of the drums, and
the chants of our ancestors,
singing courage into our
bodies, to give us the
strength to hold that space
for each other.

And in that moment, when
we're connected to the
divine-- our power source,
all the shades of Browns will
yell out brighter than the
sun.

And everyone will be silent...
unable to say: "I don't see
color" again.

Quien soy?

I am the conquered and
conqueror.

A confused identity infused
with the burning smells of
chiles over the comal-
sprinkled over the pozole at
Navidad and blended into
the spices of horchata and
rompope, sweet enough to
digest and welcome into
your mouths over and over
again.

Blanquita, gringuita, quien
soy?

From posadas to pep rallies.

Quien soy?

Conquered and conqueror,
mixed into one. Snow white
skin of the conqueror,
charcoal black hair and a
Brown heart of the
conquered.

Grandma's blue eyes and
blond hair telling me the
secret recipes of her pueblo
at dinner next to the rosca.
Her Spanish accent tingles
over my skin and takes on a
sweet scent that encourages
me into believing: I am
nothing short of magic.

Soy magia.

Sinai

Esto que ves… soy yo.
Ni mas, ni menos.
Un pedazo de ser.
Un trozo de humanidad.
Un monton de rizas.
Una pizca de locura.
Una mujer,
A veces niña,
A veces pasion,
Tal vez hasta pervercion,
Pero ay que ternura detrás de
esta Sinai.

Brown Boy

Brown boy,

You're allergic to the sun,
but your skin shouts like
you've been in a long term
love affair that I want to be a
part of.

You're the color I spent so
many summers trying to
be... but the mirror spilled
out the truth beside me.

I've floated up to the clouds
in the sky, close to you, but
hidden and shy.

Hug me, kiss me, cover me in
your warm glow. Be mine.

Cloak me in your sunshine.
I want to wake up with tan
thoughts of you and me.

Sleeping Awake

It's in those moments of deep
unconsciousness that your
deepest desires sprout up
next to me with new life and
hope.

It's just you and me.
Sleeping awake.

Naked and unashamed.

In our truths, where blue and
pink are one.

Where labels and roles are
put away.

Let's stay here, where it's
safe.

Just you and me.
Sleeping awake.

Unspoken Words

I couldn't sleep that night. It
was too hot.
I traced my fingers over the
edges of his perfectly formed
abs.

The hairs on his skin
prickling my fingertips like
thorns.

My breath shallow... holding
onto unspoken words.

My tears hit his chest, hot
and heavy, like summer
night rain on pavement.

I opened my mouth to ask
him a question: What do you
want? I said.

He responded: I don't know.

So I asked him: What does
your heart want?

He leaned his head over to
mine kissing my forehead
and wrapping his arms
around me as if he was my
blanket, the one I'd always
welcome even in 90 degree
heat, especially if he'd tell me
exactly what my soul ached
to hear: "YOU", he said,
before nodding off back to
sleep.

Read Me

She was a book... and he put
her on a bookshelf instead of
diving into the stories she
had to tell.

The art inside each page
came to life every night
whether he read her or not.

She didn't wait to author
new narratives...instead
jumped out becoming both
writer and reader.

Fairy Tale

I'm that small impressionable
child sitting by the TV,
watching cartoons and eating
cereal because it's sweeter
than growing up to be me.

Shoved into believing happy
endings come by marriage
and castles.

Stuck in a storybook where
deceitful crows and warlocks
and witches chase me down,
thirsty for a taste of my
magic.

With a carriage of curiosity,
unable to explore, restricted
and bound to gender
pronouns of she and her.

Forced to choose labels that
don't define the intricate
parts of the enchantment
within, waiting to be free and
to finally accept all of me.

27

I was 27 when I realized that
boys wanted more than what
was between my legs...

They wanted my energy...
my life force.

I searched for my power in
stories--the fairy tales I had
seen in cartoons.

But I looked for the one
where SHE saves herself.

With no books to teach me
how to slay the dragon, I
stood lost in a dim abyss.

There were others there
stuck too, immobile, frozen,
cursed.

But there was just enough
glow in my smile for him to
notice me in the darkness.

A Brown knight in a pink
cape that I had not seen in
these tales of love before.

He uttered story lines that I
knew couldn't be real.

He needed to be saved too.
We wandered and stumbled
on together, trying to save
one another from the
creatures in our past that
villainized us.

And as our way out became
clear- a sense of relief and
empty weight, of the
unknown, followed us out.

I was 27.

Wine Wednesdays

The floral berry accents
tickled every taste bud on
my tongue.

I craved more than the plum
red drink in my hand.

I wanted a burst of colors.

A palette only he could help
me paint with.

I was a canvas anxiously
awaiting the stroke of his
brush.

But I was also the painter
that night… and every night
after that.

I had one color. Red. Like an
apple.

The forbidden fruit that
called my name.

I wanted to taste it and peel
the skin as if undressing
parts of him that no one had
seen before.

Sinful thoughts filled my
wine glass in a swirl of
fantasies ready to bring my
doodles to life...but I wasn't
ready.

Swipe Right

Thank you for writing me a
whimsical whisper of hope.

For giving me a tight
embrace that soothed my
soul.

For the delicious experiences
shared over wine and staying
up past nine.

Thank you for the sweaty
nights that led to smeared
lipstick outside of Rich's.

But most of all for finally
letting me call you mine.

Quiero

Quiero correr sin tropezar en
las imágenes de su rostro.

Quiero beber hasta ya no
poder sentir su calor.

Quiero que me quieran como
yo lo quise a él.

No quiero estar sola.

Porque en mi soledad brotan
los recuerdos que formamos
cada Navidad.

Quiero sonreír y saber que
alguien me espera para
reparar lo que quebró dentro
de mi.

Y así termina nuestro cuento
de amor. En odio…Quiero
ser feliz. Pero lo odio.

Dad

Dad.
You left me.

I feel abandoned every time
my friends cancel plans and
promises are broken.

But what hurts most is
having to beg for love from
others. Feeling like I have to
fix and deny their rejection to
try and salvage some part of
our relationship that crashed
and burned long ago.

You didn't care for me the
way that I deserved and I let
others treat me in the same
way that you did.

Your selfish touch erupted
streams of lava out of my
eyes, each time you didn't
show up. I'd be scorched
with the memories of a 6
year-old girl waiting on the
balcony trying to catch a
glimpse of her dad, but end
up with nothing but ash and
burn marks, because you'd
never come.

Self-Love

There are invisible scars on
my body that are the
remnants of something I
called love.

I had become too good at
making excuses for others.

The lies started when I was
too afraid to be alone.

I was three, when I chased
after the first man I ever
loved, my father.

He imprinted in me early on
my responsibility to make
him notice me- or he would
forget all about me.

If I didn't reach out, he'd go
months or years without
calling, writing or visiting
me.

I hated myself for chasing
men and repeating this cycle
over and over again when I
grew up, but it was all I
knew.

Self-love starts with a small
seed of awareness and a
lifetime commitment to
water the wonders inside
you, and learning to redirect
your energy to heal toxic
behaviors stemming from
childhood.

And though self-love starts
within you, it can't be done
alone. It is not a linear path
because you are woven in
relationships, which are
messy, but beautiful. Allow
others a chance to see you,
because THAT will
ultimately heal you.

Silent

Like sleeping beauty
pricking herself on the
spinning wheel, my body
went numb from the bee
sting.

I was helpless, laying there
half-asleep, easy for them to
manipulate.

I stood still and lifeless; like a
wilted flower with bright
yellow petals struggling to
stay invisible.

So I went silent instead.

And when more bees came
to suckle life out of me, the
sweet nectar on my cheeks
dripped with honey to wake
me up.

I dug into my core that night
to say "NO!". And it wasn't
true love's kiss that saved
me, but my roar.

When Friendships Die

I wasn't ready when my
friendships died-rosebud
memories reduced to seeds.

The grass is greener when
you're not here. The ants and
birds in the trees run free.

I've dug up the roots to trim
and grow and hope for new
life where you use to sow.

My little green arms extend
with excitement to welcome
the beams of the sun and I
finally feel whole.

Ready for a fruitful display
of flavors and daisies to call
my friends. I'm ready to be
soiled in every single way.

My Back

My back is a fortress. Strong
enough to withstand the
shadows trying to break
through, but soft enough to
lay your head on at night.

My back is a fortress.

Built from generations of
powerful Brown men and
womxn that redefined
strength and sacrificed parts
of themselves so that I could
carry less on my back and
keep moving forward.

My back is a fortress.

Ready to protect, love and
build. And I'll smile knowing
my back is a fortress made
just for me.

Mis Pies

Mis pies quieren caminar sin
rumbo hasta encontrarte.

Toma mi mano y no me dejes
ir.
Llévame tras tus
pensamientos.
Llename de besitos.
Guia mis labios sobre tu
cuello.
Quiero que seas mio y yo
seré tuya.

Prometeme que me llevaras
hasta el fin del
mundo.Viajaremos y
bailaremos sin cesar. Mis
piesitos estan listos para una
nueva aventura.

Quieres ser mi guia?

Choices

The relationship I'm in now,
it's not the product of true
love or soul mates, but
instead of conscious
decisions to choose each
other over and over again.

It was hard and exhausting
to cycle through horrible
habits together, but
something in them felt so
good and familiar...that's
because we'd been taught
them from people we loved
and trusted so much, that it
felt okay to hurt each other in
the same way.

We had to intentionally
break into parts of ourselves
we hadn't visited in a while
to fully learn how to heal.

And honestly it felt like
digging into a wound that
had recently scabbed.

What helped me be with you
was thinking back...And
what are the odds that you
happened to me? It was a
choice to be in the pain, but
also to talk about it and listen
to everything you said. And
we're not hurting each other
anymore... the bad things
are dead.

And I choose you forever.

An Ode to Badass Mujeres

Girl,

You're a badass! Those
scrapes and scars prove it…

It means that through the
pain you know how to
endure and persevere. Fall
and fall again, but push
forward mujer. Let's go!

Sigue adelante. No estas sola.
I'm here.

Artist, activist, teacher,
mother, you inspire me.

Generations are watching
con la boca abierta y un poco
de babita.

Look at you! Como brillas
estrellita, from the hoods to
the courtroom, not as a
criminal, but as the lawyer.

De los barrios de California a
Tejas, you light up a sky map
that sings through the
stereotypes and
microaggressions of our
Brown people and pounds
the gavel on oppression and
injustice.

Gracias amiga!
You're such a badass mujer!!

Please enjoy the following coloring pages.

They're fun snapshot moments that bring me joy. Disfruta!

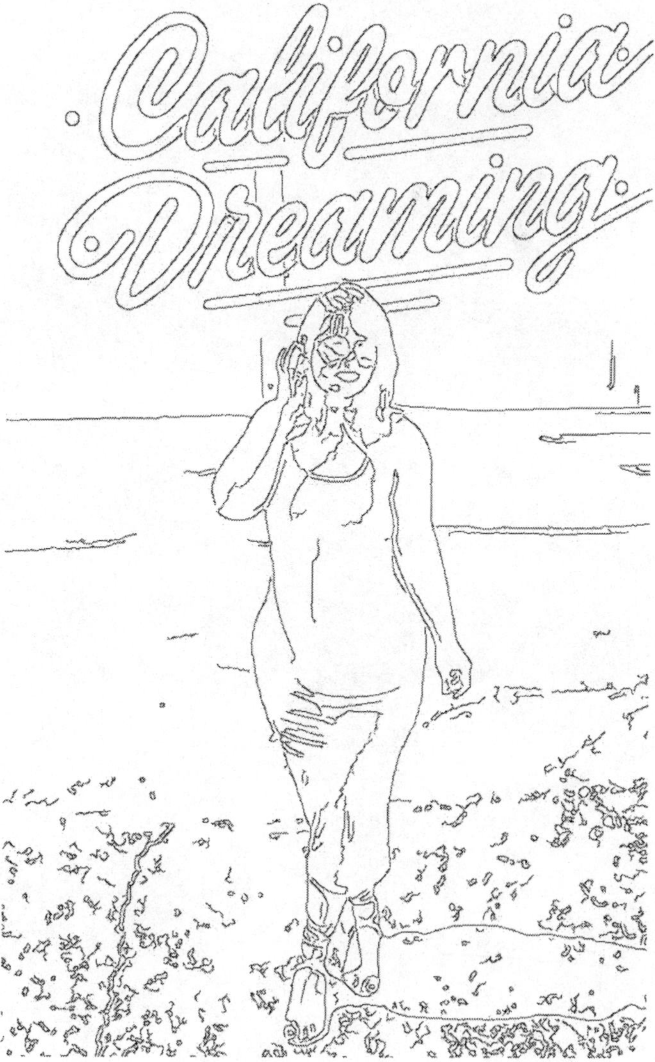
California
Dreaming

YOU
GO,
GIRL

These blank pages are for you.
Write, draw, sing or scream.
And never forget how much power you have.

Made in the USA
San Bernardino, CA
25 July 2020

76004176R00044